THE LITANY
OF THE SACRED HEART

D1598765

THE LITANY
OF THE
SACRED HEART

Mario Collantes

•

Illustrated

CATHOLIC BOOK PUBLISHING CORP.
New Jersey

Contents

NIHIL OBSTAT: Rev. Msgr. James M. Cafone, M.A., S.T.D.
Censor Librorum

IMPRIMATUR: ✠ Most Rev. John J. Myers, J.C.D., D.D.
Archbishop of Newark

The Nihil Obstat and Imprimatur are official declarations that a book or pamphlet is free of doctrinal or moral error. No implication is contained therein that those who have granted the Nihil Obstat and Imprimatur agree with the contents, opinions or statements expressed.

(T-374)

ISBN 978-0-89942-366-1

Originally published by, and copyrighted to, Word & Life Publications, Makati, Metro Manila, Philippines, in 2008.

Printed in Hong Kong
www.catholicbookpublishing.com

A Brief Introduction

The Litany of the Sacred Heart of Jesus is one of the four officially approved litanies in use in the Western rites of the Catholic Church. (The other three are the Litanies of the Saints, of Loreto, and of the Name of Jesus). The Litany of the Sacred Heart is by far the second most widely used, after the Litany of Loreto, or "Litany of the Blessed Virgin Mary."

A Litany of the Sacred Heart has been used, with some variations in the content and number of invocations, since the seventeenth century. Over the past three centuries, it has been a valid instrument in nourishing and expressing the love of millions of devotees for Jesus, under the title of "Sacred Heart."

WHAT IS A "LITANY"?

A "litany" is a form of prayer that has been in use in the Catholic Church as early as the sixth century. Essentially, it consists of a series of supplications addressed to God and some Saints. It is characterized by the brief character of the invocations and by the alternation of invocations (uttered by a member of the clergy or a prayer leader) and an equally brief response recited or sung by the people.

All litanies have the basic following structure:

- A series of invocations directed to the Blessed Trinity and each of the three Divine Persons, to which the people respond: "Have mercy on us!"

- Then a series of invocations addressed to Mary Most Holy or other Saints follows, and to which the people respond: "Pray for us!"

- Every litany ends with a series of invocations addressed to Jesus as the Lamb of God, and to the Triune God. To each of these final invocations the people respond: "Hear us!" or "Graciously, hear us!"

HOW THE LITANY OF THE SACRED HEART ORIGINATED

Historians tell us that private forms of invocations addressed to the Sacred Heart of Jesus existed even before St. Margaret Mary Alacoque. Initially, those collections of invocations were used mostly within monasteries of the Visitation, the religious congregation of nuns that had been established by St. Francis de Sales and St. Jane Frances de Chantal, and of which Sr. Margaret Mary Alacoque was a member. Some of those litanies were quite similar to the one with which we are familiar and date back to the time of St. Margaret Mary, the

Saint who is closely connected with the devotion to the Sacred Heart of Jesus. One of those litanies was composed by Sr. Yoly (of the Visitation Monastery of Dijon). Another one was the work of Mother de Soudeilles, superior of the Visitation Monastery of Moulins. A third litany was composed by Fr. Jean Croiset, who was the spiritual director of Sr. Margaret Mary after the death of St. Claude de la Colombière.

A common feature of these three litanies was that they consisted of thirty-three invocations in honor of the Sacred Heart (thirty-three being the number of years of Our Lord on earth).

A fourth litany, which consisted of twenty-seven invocations culled from the three already mentioned, was composed by Sr. Anna Maddalena de Ramuzat of the Visitation Monastery of Marseilles, a city in southern France. That litany was recited by the people of that city in 1720 during the terrible plague that was decimating the population. As the people recited or sang the litany, the plague did abate and eventually ceased altogether—a miraculous event, which everybody in Marseilles attributed to the intervention of the Sacred Heart.

More than one and a half centuries later, the bishops of Marseilles and Autun petitioned the Pope to officially approve the litany in honor of the Sacred Heart used in their respective dioceses. Since the two litanies varied in several points, the Congregation of the Rites produced a "unified version," which was the fruit of several modifications and a few additions. That unified version consisted of thirty-three invocations and became the "official" Litany in honor of the Sacred Heart. Pope Leo XIII approved it for use in the whole Church on April 2, 1899.

THE STRUCTURE OF THE LITANY OF THE SACRED HEART

The thirty-three invocations that make up the "body" of the Litany of the Sacred Heart are not a random sequence but can be grouped into two major parts. The first part consists of 16 invocations that concern the relationship of the Sacred Heart with the Blessed Trinity and about Jesus as God's Incarnate Son. The second part (17-33) focuses on Jesus' relationship to mankind. Within these two parts, further subdivisions or "clusters" of invocations are possible, which focus more sharply on different aspects or relationships of the Sacred Heart. Below is an example of a more detailed classification of the invocations:

• The *first cluster* (1-3) presents the relationship of the Sacred Heart to each of the three Divine Persons of the Holy Trinity;

- The *second* (4-7) focuses on Jesus as true God;

- The *third* (8-16) describes qualities of Jesus as true Man;

- The *fourth* (17-33) is the longest and focuses on what Jesus is or has done for us.

Other divisions and clusterings are possible, and since we do not know what structure was followed by those who composed the Litany, everyone is free to follow one's judgment. But these are only external and secondary aspects of the Litany. What matters is the fact that this collection of thirty-three invocations is a way to express and nurture our love for the Person of Jesus Who is the source of our salvation and hope.

A WORD ABOUT THE REFLECTIONS CONTAINED IN THIS BOOK

The brief reflections that follow are by no means exhaustive or highly scholarly. Rather, they are an initial attempt to bring out some of the immense richness of the content of each invocation with a view to nourishing the personal piety of the devotees and thereby enable them to grow in their love for the Lord Jesus. Each of us can further develop and deepen these reflections, as the Spirit may guide him or her, and depending on one's personal sensitivity, past experiences, or present condition.

Litany of the Most Sacred Heart of Jesus

L ORD, have mercy.
  Christ, have mercy.
Lord, have mercy.
Christ, hear us.
Christ, graciously hear us.
God, the Father of heaven, *have mercy on us.**
God the Son, Redeemer of the world,
God, the Holy Spirit,
Holy Trinity, one God,
Heart of Jesus, Son of the eternal Father,
Heart of Jesus, formed by the Holy Spirit in the womb of the Virgin Mother,
Heart of Jesus, substantially united to the Word of God,
Heart of Jesus, of infinite majesty,
Heart of Jesus, sacred temple of God,
Heart of Jesus, tabernacle of the Most High,
Heart of Jesus, house of God and gate of heaven,
Heart of Jesus, burning furnace of charity,
Heart of Jesus, abode of justice and love,
Heart of Jesus, full of goodness and love,
Heart of Jesus, abyss of all virtues,
Heart of Jesus, most worthy of all praise,
Heart of Jesus, King and center of all hearts,

---

* *"Have mercy on us"* is repeated after each invocation.

Heart of Jesus, in Whom are all the treasures of wisdom and knowledge,

Heart of Jesus, in Whom dwells the fullness of Divinity,

Heart of Jesus, in Whom the Father was well pleased,

Heart of Jesus, of Whose fullness we have all received,

Heart of Jesus, desire of the everlasting hills,

Heart of Jesus, patient and most merciful,

Heart of Jesus, enriching all who invoke You,

Heart of Jesus, fountain of life and holiness,

Heart of Jesus, propitiation for our sins,

Heart of Jesus, loaded down with opprobrium,

Heart of Jesus, bruised for our offenses,

Heart of Jesus, obedient to death,

Heart of Jesus, pierced with a lance,

Heart of Jesus, source of all consolation,

Heart of Jesus, our life and resurrection,

Heart of Jesus, our peace and reconciliation,

Heart of Jesus, victim for our sins,

Heart of Jesus, salvation of those who trust in You,

Heart of Jesus, hope of those who die in You,

Heart of Jesus, delight of all the Saints,

Lamb of God, You take away the sins of the world; *spare us, O Lord!*

Lamb of God, You take away the sins of the world; *graciously hear us, O Lord!*

Lamb of God, You take away the sins of the world; *have mercy on us.*

℣. Jesus, meek and humble of Heart.

℟. *Make our hearts like to Yours.*

L ET us pray.
Almighty and eternal God,
look upon the Heart of Your most beloved Son
and upon the praises and satisfaction
that He offers You in the name of sinners;
and to those who implore Your mercy,
in Your great goodness, grant forgiveness in
the Name of the same Jesus Christ, Your Son,
Who lives and reigns with You forever and ever.

℟. **Amen.**

Heart of Jesus,
Son of the
Eternal Father

When we speak of the "Heart of Jesus" we mean not just His physical Heart, but especially the whole of His Person. We use the term "Heart" and the image of this vital part of a human being to symbolize Jesus' love—a love that is both human and divine. Jesus is, in fact, both Man and God.

As "Son of Man" Jesus shares in our human nature, destiny, and limitations in every way possible, except sin. But the Man Jesus is also "special" because He has no human father. He is "the Son of Mary" in all truth, but He is not really "the Son of Joseph, the carpenter." Those who thought that He was the Son of Joseph were somehow "deceived" by the fact that Jesus was born in the family of Mary and Joseph.

In reality, however, Jesus of Nazareth was "Son of Mary" and "Son of God." His Father was not a human being but the eternal God Who had generated His Personhood from all eternity and imprinted on Him all the marks of the nature, dignity, and power that are proper to God.

As we proclaim in the Nicene Creed, Jesus of Nazareth is not only human, but also "true God from true God, begotten, not made, one in being with the Father." As "the Son of the Eternal Father," Jesus loves also in a divine fashion. His physical Heart is a symbol and instrument of the Father's eternal love for each of us and for all human beings.

Heart of Jesus,
Formed by the Holy
Spirit in the Womb
of the Virgin Mary

Born of woman, born under the Law, Jesus, "the Son of Man," has the roots of His humanity in the womb of the Blessed Virgin Mary, who, by God's grace, had been preserved from original sin from the moment of her conception. Like a fertile field, the Immaculate Virgin produced the humanity of Jesus not through the intervention of an earthly father, but through the Holy Spirit. Jesus, therefore, is not the fruit of two human loves but of the primordial, eternal love of the Holy Spirit and of the immaculate, virginal love of Mary Most Holy.

Molded by the Holy Spirit, Jesus' sacred humanity was endowed with an extremely acute intelligence that could penetrate the mysteries of God and of man's heart; a most pure affectivity, capable of encompassing all human beings; a deep compassion for those who were afflicted in their body or soul; a perfect Will, constantly bent on carrying out the Father's plan.

As His Mother, Mary gave Jesus the very best all mothers give their children: she taught Him to speak, to pray, to relate to others with respect and love; she molded Him into the perfect "Son of Man" with all the wonderful traits that made Him the delight of all those who knew Him.

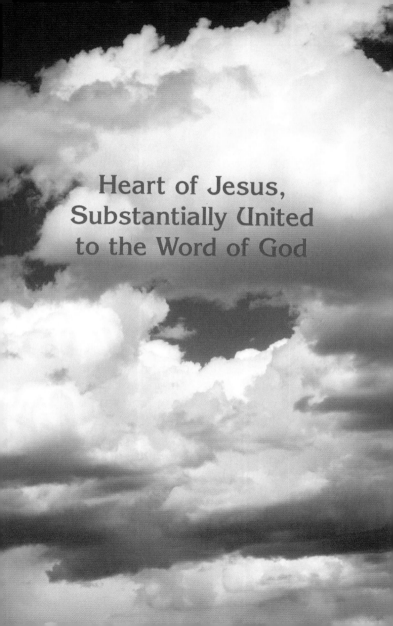

Heart of Jesus,
Substantially United
to the Word of God

Jesus of Nazareth, the Son of the Virgin Mary, and the eternal Word of God, the Son of the Father, is not two persons, but one: the second Person of the Blessed Trinity. The two natures, in Jesus, are substantially united, though remaining distinct. Jesus is 100% Man and 100% God. This is what qualifies Him to be the Redeemer of mankind.

The love of the Heart of Jesus is human love at its best as it pours itself on all those who are the objects of His attention and affection: the sick, the sorrowful, the rejected, the poor—all those who have been in any way victimized by Satan. His "humanness" makes Him also vulnerable to disappointments, rejection, ingratitude, betrayal, desertion. . . . These are consequences of His being fully human.

His substantial unity with the Word of God, on the other hand, has given an immense value to all that the Heart of Jesus and His love have cherished, blessed, and endured. As John Paul II stated, "In Jesus, God loves humanly, suffers in a human manner, and rejoices in a human way. And vice versa, in Jesus human love, human suffering, and human glory acquire a divine intensity and power." This is why just one single act of love of the Heart of Jesus is sufficient to save the entire universe. And we rejoice in being loved so dearly.

Heart of Jesus,
Infinite of Majesty

At the Incarnation, the eternal Son of the Father divested Himself of the splendor of divinity and took the form of a slave. In the words of the Apostle Paul, "Though He was in the form of God, He did not regard equality with God something to be grasped. Rather, He emptied Himself, taking the form of a slave, being born in human likeness. Being found in appearance as a man, He humbled Himself, and became obedient to death, even death on a Cross" *(Phil 2:6-8).* Centuries earlier, the Prophet Isaiah had stated, "He was . . . a Man of sorrows Who was no stranger to suffering. . . . One from Whom men avert their gaze. . . . Although it was our afflictions that He bore" *(Isa 53:3-4).*

He did all that, not out of necessity, but out of love. All along, however, the divine power of the Trinity remained in Him, hidden as it were, like a treasure buried in a field. So did His glory and His majesty. Occasionally, however, His hidden greatness manifested itself in the miracles He worked, the sins He forgave, and especially in the refulgence of His Transfiguration.

The revelation of the divine power and majesty that were inherent in Jesus and His Heart found its climax in the Resurrection. It was on that occasion that Jesus' infinite majesty and glory shattered the power of death, not only for Himself, but also for the whole of humankind.

Heart of Jesus,
Sacred Temple of God

The whole universe is God's temple. All His creatures within it give praise and honor to Him. The temple built in Jerusalem was meant also to be a reminder of this, as well as to encourage all the members of the Chosen People to become the visible manifestation of the universe at prayer.

But more precious than any material temple is the heart of every human being. Each human heart is meant to be the temple of living flesh, where God is praised, thanked, loved, and adored. But of all human hearts, none can equal the Heart of Jesus. The other two Persons of the Blessed Trinity dwelt in it in the most perfect way, permeating every fiber of it. And every fiber of the human Heart of Jesus worshiped the Father and the Spirit in the most perfect manner.

This is what makes Jesus "the perfect Worshiper." This is what makes His Heart "God's dwelling . . . with mankind" *(Rev 21:3).* And in Him God's presence sanctifies all of mankind.

As devotees of the Sacred Heart we should do our best every day to reproduce in our hearts the traits and love of our sublime Model.

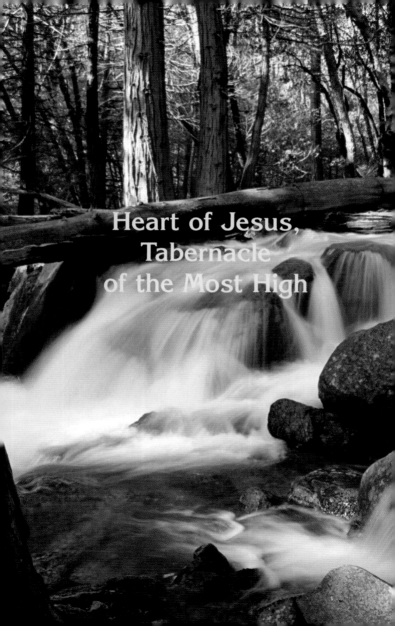

Heart of Jesus,
Tabernacle
of the Most High

The original "tabernacle" was the tent built by Moses in the desert as the Israelites journeyed and sojourned in the desert while they were on the way to the Promised Land. Within the tent was the Ark of the Covenant, which contained the two tablets of the Law. The Ark was meant to be the constant reminder of God's presence among His people. The tent was the sacred place where Moses could talk to God directly, present to Him the requests of the people, and receive from Him the instructions to be communicated to the people.

When He took flesh and became a human being, God's eternal Son "pitched His tent ('tabernacle') among us" *(Jn 1:14)*. This means that He came to share in the frailty of our nature, while at the same time becoming "the Tabernacle" of the Most High, the most holy sign of God's presence in our midst.

By a unique combination of roles, Jesus of Nazareth is both the sacred Tabernacle, erected by God Himself in the desert of human history, and the new Mediator of the everlasting Covenant, the One Who brings to the Father the pleas of all His brethren and conveys to them the wishes and blessings of the Father.

Heart of Jesus,
House of God
and Gate of Heaven

Jesus is not only God's Temple and Tabernacle, but also His "House" and the "Gate of Heaven." These are two interconnected aspects and functions of the same reality: the Person of Jesus Christ.

The term "House" connotes something visible, something over which God can claim uncontested property; a "place" in which God dwells in the fullness of His Being, and where He feels perfectly at home. Such is the heart of Jesus, the perfect "House of God."

But Jesus is also the "Gate of Heaven"—the only One through Whom mankind can enter the Kingdom of eternal bliss. There is no other gate to heaven, for Jesus is the only Redeemer and Savior of humankind. He has no equals. He has no competitors. Jesus solemnly proclaimed Himself to be "THE GATE" through which the sheep can enter into the security of the fold or through which they exit to enjoy the pastures of the divine meadows. This is why we acclaim Him as the only Gate of Heaven.

And we, the sheep and lambs of God's flock, should be eternally grateful to Jesus for being our Gate to the rich meadows of God's grace and the tranquility of God's house.

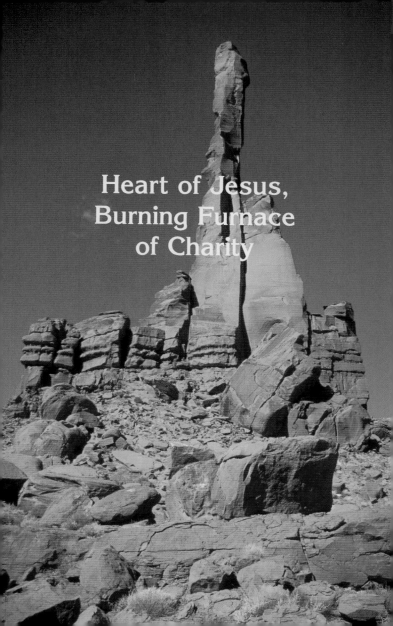

Heart of Jesus,
Burning Furnace
of Charity

There are different forms of fire and different, likewise, are the results of these fires. There is a fire that destroys even the best in us: it is the fire of impure passions, greed, pride, aggressiveness. . . . These are the fires of death. They lead to the fires of hell. Jesus has nothing to do with these types of fire.

There is also a fire that burns impurities and garbage, a fire that purifies precious metals or melts them, thereby making them beautiful and useful. This "benevolent fire" is a symbol of the fire of love that purifies, refines, sublimates, and transforms people into better persons. It is the fire that has its origin in the Heart of Jesus and is like a furnace burning with boundless charity.

This charity never ceases burning, not even in front of the coldest forms of rejection and offenses, for it is the charity/love that is immensely greater than human ingratitude and sinfulness. This is why the fire of love that burns within the furnace of the Heart of Jesus can consume the hugeness of our moral miseries and shortcomings, purifying our hearts from whatever defiles them or makes them lose the luster they were meant to have. This is the "holy fire" that the Holy Spirit ignited in the hearts of Mary and all the Saints, the fire that warms up and moves to action the souls that are frigid or crippled by callous indifference to the immense tragedies that afflict mankind.

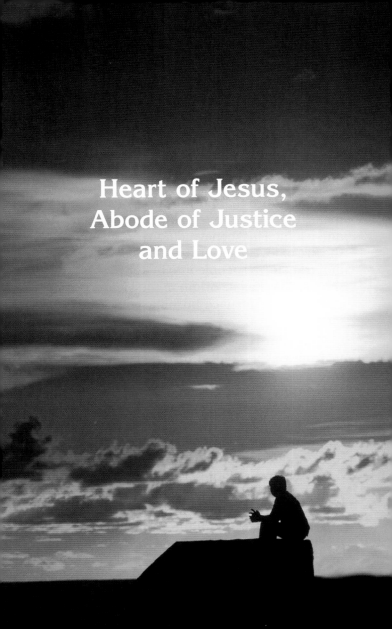

Heart of Jesus,
Abode of Justice
and Love

Justice is one of the attributes of God. He is the Just One who rewards each individual according to his or her deeds. But if God were only Justice, we would all be doomed, for no creature can measure up to the demands of Divine Justice. God, however, is also perfect Love. In Him, justice and love meet, complement, and further perfect each other, as it were. It is this blending of Justice and Love in God that is the origin and guarantee of our "justification"—the pure gift that no one can deserve; the absolutely free gift that makes us "just" in God's sight.

In the mystery of the Incarnation, God's Justice and Love have found in the Heart of Jesus their perfect revelation and actualization. He is the vessel from which our justification and salvation overflow. That is why Jesus is the only source of our hope, our redemption and sanctification.

As the human abode of God's Justice and Love, the Heart of Jesus is also the perfect Model we should do our best to reproduce. From Him we should also derive inspiration on how to treat our neighbor, by harmonizing the demands of justice with the balm of love. We will thereby make up for our endless failures in justice and love.

Heart of Jesus,
Full of Goodness
and Love

Goodness and loving kindness were the most outstanding traits of Jesus' personality, behavior, and teaching. They were the clearest revelation of what God is like. "No one has ever seen God," writes the Apostle John. And he continues, "It is the only Son, [Who is] God, Who is at the Father's side, Who has made Him known" *(Jn 1:18)*.

This is why people came to see in Jesus how immensely good and loving God is, to the good and the bad alike, for He is Father to all. It was from Jesus' Heart, filled with the Father's goodness and love, that His deeds of compassion, mercy, and forgiveness overflowed like an inexhaustible life-giving stream. It was such a superabundance of goodness and love that led Jesus to show so much care for the poor, the sick, the lonely, the hungry, the thirsty, the weak, the sorrowing, and the sorrowful. He never turned away anyone who went to Him, not even the greatest sinners, as Mary Magdalene, the repentant thief, and so many Saints can testify.

This is the fundamental attitude and behavior that each of us should always endeavor to imitate, that our frail hearts and lives, too, may be full of goodness and love.

Heart of Jesus,
Abyss
of All Virtues

In the life of a person, virtues are like streams of fresh water that delight the eye and make the surrounding area lush and fertile. The life and prosperity of a certain region depend to a great extent on the presence of such streams. But it can happen that streams of material water may gradually or even abruptly dry up. The devastating consequences of such a loss are soon visible and terrible. They spell misery for vegetation, animals, and people.

All the virtues that enrich our lives derive from the Heart of Jesus as from their main source—a source that will never dry up. All virtues gush forth from Him for He, as the Incarnate Son of God, is the source of all good. There is no other. Any attempt to find "alternative sources" of outstanding moral/spiritual qualities (for this is what virtues are), is destined to fail. Only in the Heart of Jesus do all virtues find their origin and the nourishment that ensures their preservation and development.

Indeed, if we want to progress in our moral and spiritual life and thereby grow in holiness, we have to draw closer and closer to the Heart of Jesus. From our intimacy with Him we will derive the freshness and vital energy that fill our existence with virtuous thoughts, aspirations, and actions. Such has been the experience of all the Saints, starting with Mary Most Holy.

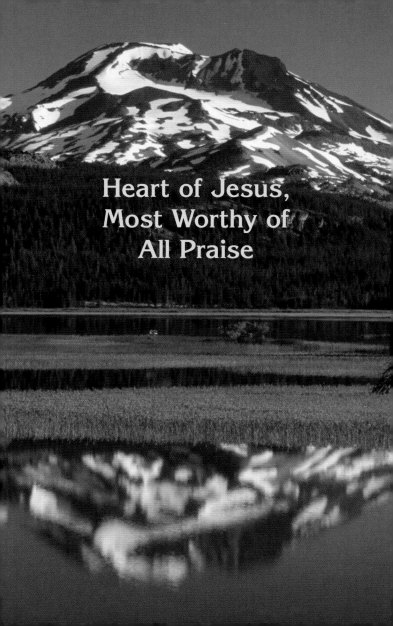

Heart of Jesus,
Most Worthy of
All Praise

People are rightly praised for their achievements. The most outstanding ones are given prestigious awards. Their names are engraved in markers and monuments. Of all the "awardees," no one is worthier than Jesus. Nay, no one can match Him, for He did everything perfectly.

"He has done everything well!" proclaimed the crowds when they witnessed the wonderful miracles He was performing, as He cleansed the lepers, gave sight to the blind, speech to the dumb, agility to the crippled, and even restored life to the dead. But all the miracles that He performed were still nothing in comparison with the "wonder of wonders" that is the salvation of mankind—a salvation Jesus brought about through His Passion, death, and Resurrection, and which is constantly and universally made present through the Sacraments, but especially through the Eucharist.

It is in the sacrament of Christ's love that His Heart reveals all its "resourcefulness" and perfection, as it encapsulates His Divinity and humanity in the simplicity of bread and wine, which possess the unique power to nourish souls, transform, energize, and inspire lives. Rightly we acknowledge this "living wonder" as we sing, "O Sacrament most Holy, O Sacrament Divine, all praise and all thanksgiving be every moment thine!"

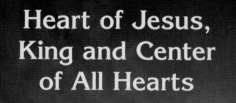

Heart of Jesus,
King and Center
of All Hearts

Jesus never claimed the title "King," though no one more than He deserved it. But He was, indeed, King, since He was the Son of the King of the universe, and to Him the Father had given all authority and power.

He implied His royal dignity in some of His parables in which He spoke of the "Son of Man" (that is: Himself) as the One Who would come in glory to judge all human beings. This will take place at the end of time, in the majesty and glory that will characterize that decisive moment of human history. But it was on Calvary that Jesus revealed the "Kingly love" of His Heart.

There, a poor human wreck—the repentant thief—proclaimed aloud his faith in the Kingship of Christ. And He, the innocent crucified "Lord Jesus," exercised the divine power of His love by promising heaven to the repentant crucified sinner, who represented all sinful humankind. It was from the Cross that Christ proclaimed His Kingship and exercised it as no simple mortal man could do. It was the unmatchable love of His Heart that brought Jesus to endure the mockery of being crowned not with a gold crown but with a crown of thorns. It was His Kingly love for us that brought Him to embrace the Cross as the most precious of all thrones. It is to His transfixed Heart that all human hearts should direct their grateful love.

Heart of Jesus,
in Whom Are All
the Treasures of
Wisdom and Knowledge

Wisdom and knowledge have always been sought after as precious treasures in all great civilizations. Outstanding among all is King Solomon, the young son of David, who, at the beginning of his reign, implored from God the gift of wisdom, rather than riches and power. In response to Solomon's prayer, the Lord God bestowed on him not only the knowledge and wisdom he had asked for, but all other blessings besides. So much so that even the Queen of the South traveled thousands of miles to be able to learn from the wisest of all kings.

Jesus is immensely greater than Solomon, as He Himself declared. He has the knowledge that surpasses every other knowledge: He knows the Father at a depth and with a clarity that no creature will ever be able to attain. And from this fundamental knowledge of the Father, Jesus derived the wisdom that enabled Him to always make the right choices—the choices that are perfectly in line with the Father's Will.

There can be no more precious treasure than this—the knowledge and wisdom we all should yearn for as devotees of the Heart of the One Who said, "Learn from Me, for I am meek and humble of heart" and "I have given you an example that just as I have done, you also may do."

Heart of Jesus,
in Whom Dwells
the Fullness
of Divinity

All creatures bear the marks of the wisdom and glory of their Creator. This is specially true of us human beings. God actually dwells in us to the extent that we can mirror His presence and attest to His wisdom and power. Jesus alone, however, is the perfect "image of the invisible God, the firstborn of all creation" *(Col 1:15)*. He "is the reflection of God's glory, and the perfect expression of His very being"*(Heb 1:3)*. This is the reason why in the Heart of Jesus, in the very core of His being, dwells the fullness of Divinity, as we proclaim in the Litany.

Due to the self-emptying effect of the Incarnation, during His earthly life, the Son of God's splendor was concealed under the ordinary appearance of a mortal man. But at His Transfiguration, the radiance of the Divinity that was in Him was revealed to some chosen disciples on Mount Tabor. That was the moment in which the fullness of the Divinity that was hidden in the Man Jesus shone in all its power and brilliance.

That was also the event that is meant to be our constant inspiration and aspiration. For this is our calling and our challenge: to allow God to permeate our being ever more deeply that ever more clearly we may reflect the splendor of the Heart of Jesus.

Heart of Jesus,
in Whom the Father
Was Well Pleased

Twice did the Father declare that He was well pleased with His Son Jesus: at the Jordan and on Mount Tabor. But those two occasions were only the "tips of the iceberg," as it were. The entire life of Jesus was a constant source of pleasure and satisfaction for His heavenly Father. Jesus was always eager to do the Father's Will to the point of accepting to die on the Cross in fulfillment of the divine plan of salvation. That was the highest test, and Jesus passed it with flying colors.

How different was the situation in the history of mankind when people who had received so much from God dared to ignore His clear orders and to prefer, instead, to follow the devil's temptation! From the Garden of Eden to the latest crime committed on the surface of the earth, we have an endless string of rebellions against God.

And we are part of that ugly chain of cases of unfaithfulness. We belong to the crowd of those who have displeased God. If we want to hear the consoling, affirming sentence, "You are My child, in whom I am well pleased," we have only one thing to do: imitate the example of our perfect Model, Jesus, the faithful Servant and Son. Then will the Father be pleased with us, too!

Heart of Jesus,
of Whose Fullness
We Have All Received

One of the great worries of the industrial-ized world is the gradual decrease of non-renewable sources of energy, such as oil and coal. No matter how vast the deposits of these nonrenewable sources of energy may be, everybody knows that we are heading toward their depletion, with the consequent crisis this will usher in. Hence, the worry and the search for "alternative sources of energy.". . .

This fear of an end of the "great bonanza" does not apply to moral and spiritual energies. In a special manner, it does not apply to the fullness of love, grace, and life that the Heart of Jesus is. These "spiritual riches" are, indeed, the essential content of the "fullness" we are reflecting upon in this invocation.

It is the fullness that John talks about at the beginning of his Gospel when he proclaims that God's only Son was "full of grace and truth" and that "from His fullness we have all received" *(Jn 1:14b, 16)*. It is the fullness of "spiritual water"—the grace of the Holy Spirit—that Jesus promises the Samaritan woman *(see Jn 4:14)*. It is the fullness of life that Jesus offers to all those who believe in Him when He states, "I have come that they may have life, and have it to the full" *(Jn 10:10)*. This is the "inexhaustible fullness" with which we all have been enriched.

Heart of Jesus,
Desire of the
Everlasting Hills

L over seeks lover. It is in the nature of love to bring people to union and, when they are far apart, to intensely desire to be together and nothing makes us happier than the fulfillment of such a yearning. This is true of the love that binds human beings. It is especially true of the love that binds God and us. This is always verified with regard to God's love for us.

He wants to be close to us, to be part of our lives, our plans, our aspirations, and even our difficulties. The signs of such desire are numberless for those who know how to read the alphabet of God's communication to us. The greatest and clearest sign of God's love for mankind is Jesus Christ, and His Heart is the core of it all.

It is in the Heart of Jesus—a Heart afire with love, crowned with thorns, and pierced by a lance—that we have the proof of how much God loves us. That same Heart teaches us, too, how much we should love God and yearn to be united with Him. All the Saints of the past and of the present, starting with Mary Most Holy, "have learned the lesson" and lived its message with great intensity, as they constantly sought to know His love ever better and to be united with Him evermore.

Heart of Jesus,
Patient and
Most Merciful

Patience is a sign and proof of love. We can see this most eloquently in the patience that parents, and especially mothers, have with their children—the way they put up with their whims and naughtiness, and even with their occasional aggressiveness and lack of love.

God is immensely more patient with us than the most patient of all mothers because He loves us more than any mother loves her child. And Jesus, with His loving and merciful Heart, is the clearest sign of God's patient love. We see His immense patience in the way He treats His hard-headed disciples. It is especially in His attitude toward sinners and enemies that the loving patience of His Heart becomes mercy and compassion. We see that in the way He treated the sinful woman caught in adultery and the prostitute who bathed His feet with her tears, in the way He conquered Zacchaeus, in the forgiveness He extended to Peter and the other disciples who deserted Him, and in His praying for those who were crucifying Him.

Jesus wants that we, too, become as merciful as He was. He said to His disciples, "Blessed are the merciful for they will obtain mercy" (Mt 5:7).

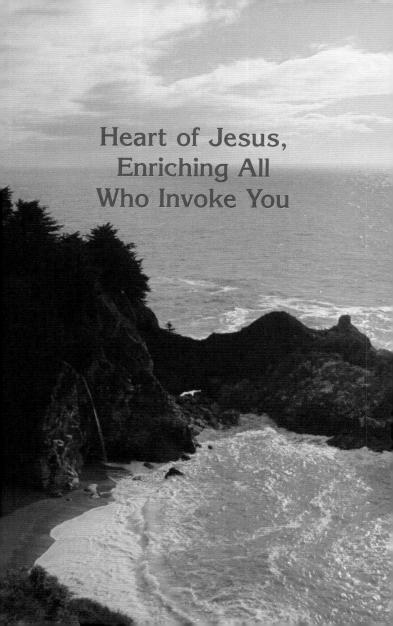

Heart of Jesus,
Enriching All
Who Invoke You

Generosity is another practical sign of love. And the most generous of all is the Lord God. He has manifested His power to enrich us by giving mankind not only the whole of creation, but also the call to live with Him forever. And when human beings forfeited that unique privilege through their sinfulness, He sent His only Son, "born of a woman, born under the Law, in order to redeem those who were under the Law . . ." *(Gal 4:4; see also Jn 3:16).*

And throughout His life, God's Incarnate Son revealed the depth of the Father's generosity by changing jars of water into exquisite wine and by feeding hungry crowds, by granting the request for healing addressed to Him by lepers and other sick people. He restored the sight to blind persons, saved His frightened disciples who were about to drown, and promised paradise to the repentant thief who was agonizing on the cross.

But the greatest signs of Christ's power to enrich us were His offering His life for the salvation of all human beings, His instituting the Eucharist, and His giving the Holy Spirit to His disciples that they might be guided to all truth, consoled in their troubles, and restored to God's grace through the ministry of the Church.

The generosity of His Heart is a constant invitation for us to do likewise.

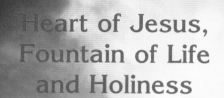

Heart of Jesus,
Fountain of Life
and Holiness

Only God is the fountain of life, as the Psalmist sings *(see Ps 36:10)*. Only God is the thrice holy, as the Cherubim in the vision of Isaiah proclaim, and as we echo in every Eucharistic celebration.

As the Incarnate Son of God, only Jesus could say in all truth, "I am . . . the life" *(Jn 11:25 and 14:6)*. Only He could challenge His opponents, "Which of you can convict Me of sin?" *(Jn 8:46)*. It was not a vain boast but the plain truth. And the source of all life and holiness in Him was His Heart, a Heart that wished to share its life and holiness with all human beings.

The whole purpose of His coming to earth was to do just that: "I have come that they may have life, and have it to the full" *(Jn 10:10)*. This much we can glance from His conversation with the Samaritan woman by the well of Jacob *(see Jn 4:14)* and in Jerusalem when He proclaimed, "Whoever believes in Me, . . . 'Streams of living water shall flow from within him' " *(Jn 7:38)*. Jesus was speaking of the Holy Spirit, notes the Evangelist, the divine Gift of the Risen Christ, Who would transform those who receive Him—all of us!—into channels of life and holiness, which would benefit our neighbor and thereby lead them back to the Fountain of all Life and Holiness.

Heart of Jesus,
Propitiation for
Our Sins

Sin destroys any good relationship with God and our neighbor. It makes us repellent to God's holiness. This is what caused Him to turn or face away from us in disgust. And this is what would condemn us to everlasting unhappiness.

It is in such a hopeless situation that Jesus comes as our Redeemer and Reconciler. Through His life of perfect obedience and His total self-offering on Calvary with the most perfect love that welled up from His Heart, He made up for the transgression of all mankind. It was through His sacrifice on the Cross that Jesus atoned for our sins by shedding His innocent Blood with His most pure and universal love. This is how He became "propitiation for our sins" and His most holy and loving Heart brought the Father to look on us favorably as His beloved, forgiven children.

In heaven, Jesus continues to be "propitiation for our sins" as He constantly intercedes for all sinners with the Father (see *Rom 8:34* and *Heb 7:25*). And here on earth, the Church makes visible and effective Jesus' saving intercession every time she celebrates the Eucharistic Sacrifice. Our wholehearted participation in this act of worship and atonement enables us to benefit from the redeeming stream of grace that flows from His pierced Heart.

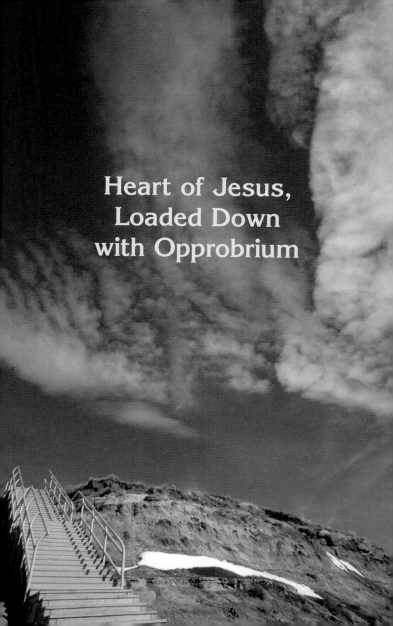
Heart of Jesus,
Loaded Down
with Opprobrium

Becoming "propitiation for our sins" cost Jesus immensely. In this invocation we reflect on how He was "loaded down with opprobrium"—that series of emotional tortures that He endured, especially during the terrible hours of His Passion.

The Roman soldiers blindfolded, hit, and shouted at Him, "Guess who has hit You!" They crowned Him with thorns and mocked, "Hail King of the Jews!" The crowd demanded, "Crucify Him and set Barabbas free!" The Jewish authorities challenged Him to come down from the Cross that they might believe in Him. . . . (See the Passion narratives of all the Gospels.) It was more than one could bear, but Jesus endured it all with boundless patience, rooted in His most loving Heart.

The Prophet Isaiah had already foreseen both the cruel treatment and the divine Victim's endurance: "He was despised. . . . We loathed Him and regarded Him as of no account, as One from Whom men avert their gaze." But, "Although harshly treated and afflicted, He did not open His mouth . . ." *(Isa 53:3, 7)*. Jesus, the Servant of Yahweh, bore all this with His forgiving love.

What a sublime example of moral strength for us when we, too, may find ourselves treated unfairly, despised, or brought down by betrayals and disappointments!

Heart of Jesus,
Bruised for
Our Offenses

Jesus did not just suffer undeservedly a series of humiliations and insults. He also suffered physically in His most pure and holy Body, which had been conceived by the power of the Holy Spirit and which had been born by the most Holy Virgin Mary. Chained and scourged mercilessly, crowned with piercing thorns, made to bear a heavy Cross, nailed to a Cross on which He hung during three endless hours . . . His whole Body was reduced to a bleeding wound!

And He was treated so cruelly not because He deserved it, but because He volunteered to take our place. He was "pierced for our offenses," that is, for our sins. "It was our afflictions that He bore," proclaimed the Prophet Isaiah centuries earlier and echoed by St. Peter: "By His wounds you have been healed" (*Isa 53:4-5* and *1 Pet 2:24*).

Jesus suffered all these torments because of all our sins. He was the only innocent One Who should not have been treated that way. We were the ones who deserved those punishments, but He volunteered to endure them in place of us. He did that not because He owed anything to us, but simply out of love—the love that overflows from His Sacred Heart!

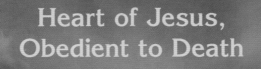

Heart of Jesus,
Obedient to Death

God's beautiful plan for mankind was thwarted, for a time, by the disobedience of Adam and Eve to His clear instruction not to eat the fruit of the tree of knowledge of good and evil. That disobedience was followed by innumerable others, and a night of suffering and frustrations engulfed the history of humankind.

Jesus came as its Holy Redeemer. His mission was to undo and make up for all the acts of disobedience of the descendants of Adam and Eve. In the Letter to the Hebrews we hear Jesus say, "You took no delight in holocausts and sin offerings. Then I said, . . . 'Behold, I have come to do Your Will, O God!' " *(Heb 10:6-7)*. In fulfillment of His mission, the whole of Jesus' life was a perfect "YES!" to the Father. In all truth He could say, "My food is to do the Will of the One Who sent Me" *(Jn 4:34)*. In the prayer He taught His disciples He included the petition, "Your Will be done, on earth as it is in heaven."

And He practiced what He taught. St. Paul synthesized Jesus' life with the sentence: "He humbled Himself, and became obedient to death, even death on a Cross" *(Phil 2:8)*. And His human career ended with the exclamation that came from the depth of His Heart: "It is finished" *(Jn 19:30)*. This is what makes Jesus the perfect example of obedience for all of us.

Heart of Jesus,
Pierced with a Lance

The Prophet Zechariah spoke about an anonymous Person who would be pierced and toward Whom people would turn their gaze in faith and wonder (see *Zec 12:10*). John, the beloved disciple, witnessed the fulfillment of that prophecy in Jesus when a soldier "thrust a lance into His side, and immediately a flow of Blood and water came forth" *(Jn 19:34)*.

That lance represented our numberless sins against God, our callousness and cruelty toward our neighbor, and our ingratitude against God's Incarnate Son. That deep wound in the side of the innocent Redeemer was the culmination of the numerous signs of supreme love He had already given on the last days of His earthly life. And from that pierced side flowed the streams of salvation made available by the Holy Spirit in the Church, especially through the Sacraments of Baptism and the Eucharist. That rivulet of Blood and water, foreshadowed in the jet of water that had gushed forth from the rock hit by Moses in the desert (see *Num 20:8-11*), would be the source of salvation and spiritual nourishment for all believers until the end of time.

And as Mary Most Holy saw the lance pierce the side of her Son, her heart was pierced, too, by the sword of compassion. Thus was the prophecy of Simeon fulfilled!

All human beings experience sadness. We have many reasons to be sorrowful because of sickness, the destructive violence of nature, the wickedness of people, and even our own moral frailty. In our loneliness, our being rejected or despised, our physical and emotional affliction, it is natural for us to seek comfort and consolation. Many try to find this in creatures. Those who are really wise seek their consolation in the Heart of Jesus, for He is the One in Whom God, the divine Consoler of His people, has found His fullest and enduring manifestation.

Throughout His life, Jesus was, indeed, a source of consolation for all the afflicted: the sick, the crippled, those who had lost a loved one, and those who were rejected by the self-righteous. In all truth, Jesus could say, "Come to Me, all you who are weary and overburdened, and I will give you rest" *(Mt 11:28)*.

And Jesus wants that we, too, become a source of consolation for all our brothers and sisters who are afflicted in one way or another. This is a challenging task, which no one would be able to fulfill without the empowerment of God's grace. That's why Jesus sent to His disciples the Holy Spirit as the divine "Consoler," in order that they and we, too, might console all those who suffer in whatever way (see *2 Cor 1:4*).

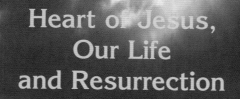

Heart of Jesus,
Our Life
and Resurrection

God has life in Himself and is the Source of all life. Jesus, the eternal Son of God, has life in Himself, too (see *Jn 5:26*), and is the Source of our life, both as our Creator and our Redeemer. When He became human, His mission was to bring us life to the full (see *Jn 10:10*), even at the cost of His own earthly life.

Jesus is the Source of our life also when we die spiritually because of our sins, for sin is, indeed, the source of our spiritual and physical death (see *Wis 2:24* and *Rom 5:12; 6:23*). Dead because of our sins, Jesus becomes our resurrection. Such was the message contained in His calling back to life the son of a widow at Nain, the daughter of Jairus, and His friend Lazarus. Such also was the message of His forgiving the sins of the paralyzed man and of the adulteress. In all truth Jesus could declare to Martha, "I am the resurrection and the life. Whoever believes in Me, even though he dies, will live" *(Jn 11:25)*.

In His power and in His Name, we have become "children of the resurrection"—spiritual resurrection from our sins and even physical resurrection at the end of time, when Jesus will defeat death forever by transforming our mortal body into the image of His own risen Body, and we will live with Him forever (see *1 Cor 15:50-55*, and *Rom 8:11*).

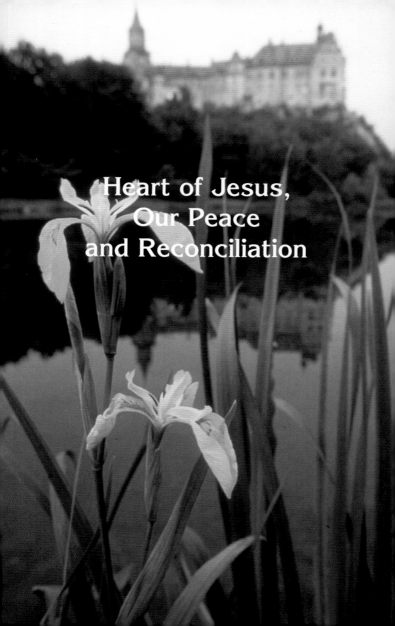

Heart of Jesus,
Our Peace
and Reconciliation

Our hearts yearn for peace. It is only when we are perfectly at peace with God, others, and ourselves that we experience perfect happiness. But this peace is endangered and destroyed by sin, for sin sets us on a collision course with God, our neighbor, and ourselves.

This is what happened to humankind with the first sin and all the other sins that followed it. This is what happens to us whenever we allow sin to rule our lives. Left to ourselves, we would never have been able to be fully at peace. It was only thanks to God's intervention that we human beings were once again able to enjoy the peace for which we yearn.

God reconciled us to Himself through His Incarnate Son Jesus Christ, the "Prince of Peace" (see *Isa 9:3-6*). His earthly birth brought peace to all men of goodwill (see *Lk 2:14*). Throughout His life, Jesus bestowed peace to so many troubled souls through His love and forgiveness. Peace was His last gift to His disciples before He died (see *Jn 14:27*). It was also His first gift to them after His Resurrection (see *Lk 24:36* and *Jn 20:19*).

He became "our peace" *(Eph 2:14)* by offering His life on the Cross to atone for our sins, and thereby achieve our reconciliation with God (see *Rom 5:10*), which is the indispensable condition for us to be also reconciled—to be at peace—with our neighbor and our very selves.

Heart of Jesus,
Victim for Our Sins

Sin is a terrible offense against God's love. It attracts the wrath of divine justice as a lightning rod attracts the destructive charges of electricity in stormy weather. All sinners deserved to suffer the just punishment due to sin, but God, in His mercy, spared them and us by allowing an innocent Victim to atone for the sins of all. The Apostle Paul expressed this dramatic and life-saving "substitution" through the most powerful sentence, "He made Him Who did not know sin to be sin for our sake, so that through Him we might become the righteousness of God" *(2 Cor 5:21).*

The coming of God's Son into this world "in the likeness of sinful flesh" was not an arbitrary imposition, but the result of His generous volunteering: "You took no delight in holocausts and sin offerings. Then I said, '. . . behold, I have come to do Your Will'" *(Heb 10:6-7).* And in Christ's self-offering to be the new and true Lamb of Sacrifice and Paschal Lamb, mankind found its salvation. His innocent and most precious Blood atoned for the sins of all and shielded sinners from the blows of the Angel of divine justice.

Jesus carries on His intercession for sinners in heaven as He stands in the presence of the Father, with the marks of His Passion. This is how He continues to be "The Lamb of God," the innocent Victim that takes away the sins of the world.

Heart of Jesus,
Salvation of Those
Who Trust in You

All human beings want to be happy. In our concrete situation as sinners, this means that we want and need to be saved from the consequences of our sinfulness and the sinfulness of other people. But salvation and happiness can come only from God. We cannot be saved by wealth, or strength, or fame, or power. We cannot be saved even by our own "good works," for no one can say, "Jesus is Lord!" without the empowering presence of the Holy Spirit. It is clear, then, that we can reach salvation only through God's grace, the fruit of His merciful love. And this salvation is made present and reaches us through the pierced Heart of His Incarnate Son, Jesus Christ.

This was made manifest especially when He met people who needed His saving intervention: the sick, the lepers, His disciples about to be drowned in the sea, or people who were in danger of being drowned by their sinfulness or the pain that afflicted their dear ones. Jesus' intervention was what made the difference every time. But every time, His saving intervention was conditioned and "unleashed," so to speak, by the faith and trust of those who needed to be saved. The repentant thief is the clearest example of this.

Trust in Jesus and in His merciful love is the condition we have to meet even today if we want to enjoy the salvation that He alone can bring.

Heart of Jesus,
Hope of Those
Who Die in You

Death has always a dark and frightening aspect, for it marks the end not only of our activities, but also of our relationship with the people dear to us. For many people death also has the dark aspect of the uncertainty about what awaits them after they have ended their earthly course.

But nothing of these fears and uncertainties should apply to those who love Jesus and believe in Him as their Lord and Savior. They know that His love is greater than human frailty and that He has prepared for His friends a "place" of endless peace, happiness, and fulfillment where they will be with Him forever (see *Jn 14:2*).

But for this "bright aspect" of death to be actualized, we have *"to die in the Lord."* This means we are to die at peace with Him, firmly believing in the Lord Jesus as the Source of all life and salvation, hoping in Him, and entrusting ourselves totally to His mercy and love. Such an attitude of total trust and hope comes spontaneously only to those who have *"lived in the Lord,"* that is: those whose earthly life has been characterized by the constant effort to do God's Will.

That is the way Jesus Himself lived and the way He died. He lived always bent on doing the Father's Will (see *Jn 4:34*). And He died by simply saying, "Father, into Your hands I commend My spirit!"

Heaven is the condition of perfect and unending happiness, the fulfillment of all our aspirations, the reward for all the good we have done, and of all the sufferings we have endured with love and faith. Heaven is the condition of peace and contentment, with no doubts or uncertainties, when all our questions will be answered and all the truths of our faith will be understood fully. In a special manner, it will be the condition of perfect communion with God and all the Saints—a condition we have in vain aspired to attain in this world. It is definitely something to look forward to.

But all these blessings will become a reality only thanks to Jesus Christ—thanks to the immense love of His Heart Who has reached to the point of volunteering to die for us and to die on a Cross, in order that we might live forever in the Kingdom that the Father has prepared for us since the foundation of the world. Heaven will be ours because of Jesus!

That is why the first thing that we will long to see upon approaching the gates of paradise will be Jesus Himself. We will yearn to contemplate the majesty of His Person, to feel the tenderness of His love, and to experience the bliss of being embraced by Him and to embrace Him as His Most Holy Mother was able to do even in her earthly life. Then will Jesus be our delight forever in the company of all the Saints.

Prayers to
the Sacred Heart*

Prayer of Union with the Sacred Heart

HAIL, Sacred Heart of Jesus,
living and strengthening source of eternal
    life,
infinite treasury of the Divinity,
and burning furnace of Divine love!
You are my refuge and sanctuary.

My loving Savior,
consume my heart in that burning love
with which Your own Heart is inflamed.
Pour out upon me the graces
that flow from Your love.
Let my heart be so united with Yours
that our wills may be one,
and my will may in all things be conformed
with Your Will.
May Your Will be the guide and rule
of my desires and of my actions.   St. Gertrude

Prayer of Self-Offering
to the Sacred Heart

O JESUS,
reveal Your Sacred Heart to me
and show me Its attractions.

* From *New Saint Joseph People's Prayerbook*, Rev.
Francis Evans, General Editor, © 2007, 2001, 1993, 1980
by Catholic Book Publishing Corp., NJ.

Unite me to It forever.
Grant that all my desires and every beat of my
       heart,
which does not cease even while I sleep,
may be a witness to You of my love
and may say to You:
Yes, Lord, I am Yours!
The pledge of my loyalty to You
rests ever in my heart
and shall never cease to be there.

Accept the little good that I do
and be pleased to make up for all my wrong-
      doing,
so that I may be able to praise You in time
as well as in eternity.

Prayer for Peace of Heart

O MOST sacred, most loving Heart of Jesus,
You are concealed in the Holy Eucharist,
and You beat for us still.
Now, as then, You say:
"With desire I have desired."
I worship You, then,
with all my best love and awe,
with fervent affection,
with my most subdued, most resolved will.
You for a while take up Your abode within me.
O make my heart beat with Your Heart!

Purify it of all that is earthly,
all that is proud and sensual,
all that is hard and cruel,

of all perversity,
of all disorder,
of all deadness.
So fill it with You,
that neither the events of the day,
nor the circumstances of the time,
may have the power to ruffle it;
but that in Your power and Your fear,
it may have peace.

Cardinal Newman

Prayer of Thanksgiving to the Father for Giving Us the Heart and Mind of Jesus

O MY God,
how great is Your love for us!
You are infinitely worthy
of being loved, praised, and glorified!
We have neither heart nor spirit worthy of
doing so.
But Your Wisdom and Goodness
have given us a way of carrying it out.
You have given us the Spirit and Heart of Your
Son,
to be our own heart and spirit,
in accord with the promise You made through
Your Prophet:
"I will give them a new heart,
I will put a new spirit in your midst" (Ezekiel
36:26).
In order that we may know
what this new heart and new spirit might be

You added:
"I will put My Spirit, which is My Heart,
in Your midst."
Only the Spirit and Heart of a God
are worthy of loving and praising a God,
of blessing and loving Him as much as He
    deserves.
Thus You have given us Your Heart,
the Heart of Your Son Jesus,
as well as the heart of His holy Mother
and the heart of the Saints, and Angels,
who together are only one heart,
as the Head and members form one single
    Body.   St. John Eudes

Prayer of Trust in the Sacred Heart

IN ALL my temptations, I place my trust in
    You,
O Sacred Heart of Jesus.
In all my weaknesses, I place my trust in You,
O Sacred Heart of Jesus.
In all my difficulties, I place my trust in You,
O Sacred Heart of Jesus.
In all my trials, I place my trust in You,
O Sacred Heart of Jesus.
In all my sorrows, I place my trust in You,
O Sacred Heart of Jesus.

In all my work, I place my trust in You,
O Sacred Heart of Jesus.
In every failure, I place my trust in You,

O Sacred Heart of Jesus.
In every discouragement, I place my trust in
    You,
O Sacred Heart of Jesus.
In life and in death, I place my trust in You,
O Sacred Heart of Jesus.
In time and in eternity, I place my trust in You,
O Sacred Heart of Jesus.

Petitions to the Sacred Heart of Jesus

LOVE of the Sacred Heart of Jesus,
    embrace my heart.
Fire of the Heart of Jesus,
inflame my heart.
Charity of the Heart of Jesus,
fill my heart.
Strength of the Heart of Jesus,
sustain my heart.
Mercy of the Heart of Jesus,
pardon my heart.
Patience of the Heart of Jesus,
do not forsake my heart.
Reign of the Heart of Jesus,
establish Yourself in my heart.
Wisdom of the Heart of Jesus,
teach my heart.
Will of the Heart of Jesus,
guide my heart.
Zeal of the Heart of Jesus,
consume my heart.

Prayer of Adoration and Petition

MOST holy Heart of Jesus,
fountain of every blessing,
I love You.
With a lively sorrow for my sins
I offer You this poor heart of mine.
Make me humble, patient, and pure,
and perfectly obedient to Your Will.

Good Jesus,
grant that I may live in You
and for You.
Protect me in the midst of danger
and comfort me in my afflictions.
Bestow on me
health of body,
assistance in temporal needs,
Your blessing on all that I do,
and the grace of a holy death.

Prayer for Response to Christ's Love

HEAVENLY Father,
we find joy in the gifts of love
that have come to us
from the Heart of Jesus, Your Son.
Open our hearts to share His life
and continue to bless us
with His love.

Heavenly Father,
we honor the Heart of Your Son

wounded by the cruelty of human beings.
That Heart is the symbol of love's triumph
and the pledge of all that human beings
are called to be.
Help us to see Christ in all whom we encounter,
and to offer Him living worship
by rendering loving service to others.

Prayer for Perseverance

O SACRED Heart of Jesus,
living and life-giving fountain of eternal
life,
infinite treasure of the Divinity,
and glowing furnace of love,
You are my refuge and my sanctuary.
O adorable and glorious Savior,
consume my heart with the burning fire
that ever inflames Your Heart.
Pour down on my soul the graces
that flow from Your love.
Let my heart be so united with Yours
that our wills may be one,
and mine may in all things be conformed to
Yours.
May Your Will be the rule
both of my desires and of my actions

St. Alphonsus Liguori

Contemporary Prayer of Reparation

L ORD Jesus Christ,
    we look at the Cross,
and we—Your pilgrim Church—can see
what sin has done to the Son of Mary,
to the Son of God.

But now You are risen and glorified.
You suffer no more in the flesh.
Sin can no longer expose You
to the Agony of the Garden,
to the Scourging,
to Death on a Cross.

But it can reach You through Your Mystical Body.
This part of You, Your Church on earth,
still feels the strength of sin.
For this we make our act of reparation.

We who have sinned in the past
now consecrate ourselves
to the healing of Your Mystical Body,
to our part in the mystery
of its well-being and its growth.
Sanctify us for this task.

May Your Sacred Heart be the symbol,
not of one love but two—
Your love for us and ours for You.
Accept our love,
and help us make it real
by serving You in our brothers and sisters,
so that love and concern may lead all people

"to know the one true God
and Jesus Christ Whom He has sent."

Apostleship of Prayer

Prayer of Consecration

I, N . . ., give myself
to the Sacred Heart of our Lord Jesus Christ,
and I consecrate to Him
my person and my life,
my actions, pains, and sufferings,
so that henceforth I shall be unwilling
to make use of any part of my being
except for the honor, love, and glory
of the Sacred Heart.

My unchanging purpose is to be all His
and to do all things for the love of Him
while renouncing with all my heart
whatever is displeasing to Him.

I take You,
O Sacred Heart,
as the object of my love,
the guardian of my life,
the assurance of my salvation,
the remedy of my weakness and inconstancy,
the atonement for all my faults,
and the sure refuge at my death.

O Heart of goodness,
be my justification before God the Father,
and turn away from me
the strokes of His righteous anger.

O Heart of love,
I place all my trust in You,
for I fear everything
from my own wickedness and frailty,
but I hope for all things
from Your goodness and bounty.

Consume in me all that can displease You
or resist Your holy Will.
Let Your pure love imprint You
so deeply upon my heart
that I shall nevermore be able to forget You
or be separated from You.
May I obtain from all Your loving kindness
the grace of having my name written in You,
for I desire to place in You
all my happiness and all my glory,
living and dying in virtual bondage to You.

St. Margaret Mary Alacoque

Charismatic Prayer of Consecration

LOVING Father in heaven,
    we come to give ourselves to You in love.
We ask You to fulfill Your promise
to give each of us a new heart.
We ask You to create in Your people
this new heart.
We praise You, Father,
for having already fulfilled this promise
in Jesus Christ, Your Son.
He is the new Heart for each of us

and for Your Church.
He is the new Heart for all people.
We ask You, Father,
to fashion our hearts after His Heart.
Give to Your Church His Heart as her new
        heart:
a heart alive and nourished by Your Spirit.
May this new heart throb with new life
throughout the Church,
as if in a new Pentecost.

May this heart beat with compassion and love
for Your poor,
for Your alienated,
for the stranger,
for the little ones.

May this heart beat with outrage for sin
and with love for the sinner.
May this heart reach out to fashion You a peo-
        ple,
born of the Spirit:
a people who will not shrink from the Cross,
even laying down their lives,
from sacrificing themselves.

Let Your people believe enough in love,
to pour themselves out for the brotherhood,
so that Your love may indeed become visible
for all to see.
May every beat of this heart
bring forth Your Kingdom.

We ask this of You,
through Christ our Lord.

Rev. J. Faber MacDonald, Pastor of St. Pius X,
Charlottetown, P.E.I.

Prayer of Family Consecration

SACRED Heart of Jesus,
    You revealed to St. Margaret Mary
Your desire to reign over Christian families.
To fulfill this desire we today proclaim
Your complete dominion over our family.
From now on we wish to live Your life,
to cultivate in our home
those virtues which bring them Your peace,
and avoid that worldliness which You have con-
    demned.
You will rule over our minds by simple faith
and over our hearts by a love
kept aflame by frequent Holy Communion.

Divine Heart of Jesus,
be pleased to preside over our family,
to bless all we do,
to dispel our troubles,
sanctify our joys,
lighten our sufferings.
If one of us should ever offend You by sin,
remind him/her,
merciful Jesus,
of Your goodness and mercy to the penitent
    sinner.
And when the hour of separation strikes,

when death brings its griefs into our midst,
those of us who go and those who must stay
will be submissive to what You have decreed.

Then it will be our consolation to remember
that the day will come when our entire family,
reunited in heaven,
will be able to sing forever
of Your glory and Your mercy.

May the Immaculate Heart of Mary
and the glorious patriarch St. Joseph
present to You this Consecration of ours
and keep us ever mindful of it
all the days of our life.
All glory to the Sacred Heart of Jesus,
our King and our Father!

American Apostleship of Prayer

Traditional Morning Offering

O JESUS,
through the Immaculate Heart of Mary,
I offer You my prayers, works, joys, and sufferings
of this day
in union with the Holy Sacrifice of the Mass
throughout the world.
I offer them
for all the intentions of Your Sacred Heart:
the salvation of souls,
reparation for sins,
the reunion of all Christians.

I offer them for the intentions of our Bishops
and of all the Apostles of Prayer,
and in particular for those
recommended by our Holy Father for this
month.

Apostleship of Prayer

Contemporary Morning Offering

ETERNAL Father,
I offer You everything I do this day:
my work, my prayers, my apostolic efforts;
my time with family and friends;
my hours of relaxation;
my difficulties, problems, distress,
which I shall try to bear with patience.

Join these my gifts to the unique offering
which Jesus Christ, Your Son, renews today
in the Eucharist.

Grant, I pray, that,
vivified by the Holy Spirit
and united to the Sacred Heart of Jesus,
my life this day may be of service
to You and to Your children
and help consecrate the world to You.

Apostleship of Prayer

Invocations in Honor
of the Sacred Heart

MAY the Sacred Heart of Jesus
be loved everywhere.

SWEET Heart of my Jesus,
grant that I may ever love You more.

SACRED Heart of Jesus,
Your Kingdom come!

DIVINE Heart of Jesus,
convert sinners,
save the dying,
and deliver the holy souls in purgatory.

SACRED Heart of Jesus,
I believe in Your love for me.

GLORY, love and thanksgiving
be to the Sacred Heart of Jesus!

O HEART of love,
I put all my trust in You;
for I fear all things from my weakness,
but I hope for all things from Your goodness.

SACRED Heart of Jesus,
have mercy on us
and on our erring brothers and sisters.

SACRED Heart of Jesus,
may You be known, loved, and imitated!

SACRED Heart of Jesus,
  protect our families.

SACRED Heart of Jesus,
  strengthened in Your Agony by an Angel,
strengthen us in our agony.

SACRED Heart of Jesus,
  let me love You and make You loved.

SACRED Heart of Jesus,
  grant that peace,
the fruit of justice and charity,
may reign throughout the world.